DUDLEY SCHOOLS
LIBRARY SERVICE

KU-455-265

Schools Library and Information Services

S00000723333

Investigate

Animal Characteristics

Sue Barraclough

Heinemann
LIBRARY

www.heinemann.co.uk/library
Visit our website to find out more information about Heinemann Library books.

To order:
☎ Phone 44 (0) 1865 888066

📄 Send a fax to 44 (0) 1865 314091

💻 Visit the Heinemann Bookshop at www.heinemann.co.uk/library to browse our catalogue and order online.

Heinemann Library is an imprint of Pearson Education Limited, a company incorporated in England and Wales having its registered office at Edinburgh Gate, Harlow, Essex, CM20 2JE – Registered company number: 00872828

Heinemann is a registered trademark of Pearson Education Limited.

Text © Pearson Education Limited 2008
First published in hardback in 2008
Paperback edition first published in 2009

The moral rights of the proprietor have been asserted.
All rights reserved. No part of this publication may be reproduced in any form or by any means (including photocopying or storing it in any medium by electronic means and whether or not transiently or incidentally to some other use of this publication) without the written permission of the copyright owner, except in accordance with the provisions of the Copyright, Designs and Patents Act 1988 or under the terms of a licence issued by the Copyright Licensing Agency, Saffron House, 6–10 Kirby Street, London EC1N 8TS (www.cla.co.uk). Applications for the copyright owner's written permission should be addressed to the publisher.

Edited by Sarah Shannon and Catherine Clarke
Designed by Joanna Hinton-Malivoire, Victoria Bevan, and Hart McLeod
Original illustrations © Pearson Education Limited 2008
Picture research by Liz Alexander
Originated by Chroma Graphics (Overseas) Pte Ltd
Printed in China by Leo Paper Group

ISBN 978 0 431932 72 9 (hardback)
12 11 10 09 08
10 9 8 7 6 5 4 3 2 1

ISBN 978 0 431932 91 0 (paperback)
13 12 11 10 09
10 9 8 7 6 5 4 3 2 1

British Library Cataloguing in Publication Data
Barraclough, Sue
 Animal characteristics. - (Investigate)
 591
A full catalogue record for this book is available from the British Library.

DUDLEY PUBLIC LIBRARIES
L ------
723333   SCH
J591·5

Acknowledgements
We would like to thank the following for permission to reproduce photographs: ©Alamy pp. **6** (Juniors Bildarchiv), **7** (STOCKFOLIO); ©FLPA pp. **11** (Jurgen & Christine Sohns), **14** (Foto Natura Stock); ©Getty Images pp. **4** (Winfried Wisniewski), **5** (Robert Harding World Imagery/Geoff Renner), **8** (Stone/Wayne R Bilenduke), **12** (Heinrich van den Berg/Gallo Images), **19** (Taxi/Thayer Syme), **22** (National Geographic / Michael S. Quinton), **25** (Taxi/Gary Randall), **27** (Taxi/Mark Conlin); ©istockphoto pp. **9**, **28** (Eric Gevaert), **10**, **28** (Christopher Withers), **20** (Kristian Sekulic); ©NHPA pp. **18** (Stephen Dalton), **24** (Andy Rouse), **26** (Rod Planck); ©Photolibrary pp. **13** (Tim Davis), **15**, **29** (Monsoon Images/ Jackson Margaret), **16** (Juniors Bildarchiv), **17**, **29** (IFA Animals), **21**, **29** (Oxford Scientific/Ian West).

Cover photograph of giraffe eating from a tall tree reproduced with permission of ©Getty Images (Art Wolfe/The Image Bank).

Every effort has been made to contact copyright holders of material reproduced in this book. Any omissions will be rectified in subsequent printings if notice is given to the publishers.

Contents

Some words are shown in bold, **like this**. You can find out what they mean by looking in the glossary.

Animal characteristics

Animals are living things. Animals eat, move and grow. There are many different types of animal. Some have fur and some have feathers. Some animals live on land and others live in water.

This seal lives in water. ➡

A characteristic is something that makes one animal different from another. For example, a bird has feathers and wings. These are characteristics of a bird.

Fur or feathers

Some animals have fur or hair on their bodies. Lions have fur. Having fur is a characteristic of a **mammal**. A lion is a mammal. Mammals are a group of animals that share certain characteristics. Mammals also feed their young on milk.

Mammals are **warm-blooded**. This means they can make heat in their bodies. Mammals live all over the world, even in very cold, icy places. Polar bears are mammals that live in cold places.

Q Why do polar bears have thick fur?

A Polar bears have thick fur to keep them warm.

8

Mammals such as apes have less hair on their bodies.
Apes usually live in warm places.

⬆ This orang-utan is a mammal.

Some animals have feathers on their body. Ducks have feathers. Having feathers is a characteristic of a bird. A duck is a bird.

Q Why do some birds have long wing feathers?

CLUE

- What can birds do that many other animals cannot?

11

A

Wing feathers help birds to fly.

Most birds can fly. Birds also have shorter, softer feathers to keep their bodies warm. Feathers can also be used to hide, or to show off to other birds.

Penguins cannot fly, but they use their wings to swim very fast.

Birds are also warm-blooded. Penguins are birds that live in cold places. A penguin has thick feathers to help it keep warm.

13

Skin or scales

Many animals do not have fur or feathers on their bodies. Animals such as snakes and lizards have dry, **scaly** skin. Snakes and lizards are **reptiles**. Dry, scaly skin is a characteristic of a reptile.

scale

Fish are covered with tiny, flat plates called scales.

Q

Why is this lizard lying in the sun?

? CLUE

• What does sunshine feel like on your skin?

A The lizard needs to warm its body in the sun so it can move.

Some animals are **cold-blooded**. This means their bodies cannot make heat. Their bodies are as cold or hot as the air or water around them. Cold-blooded animals usually live in warm places.

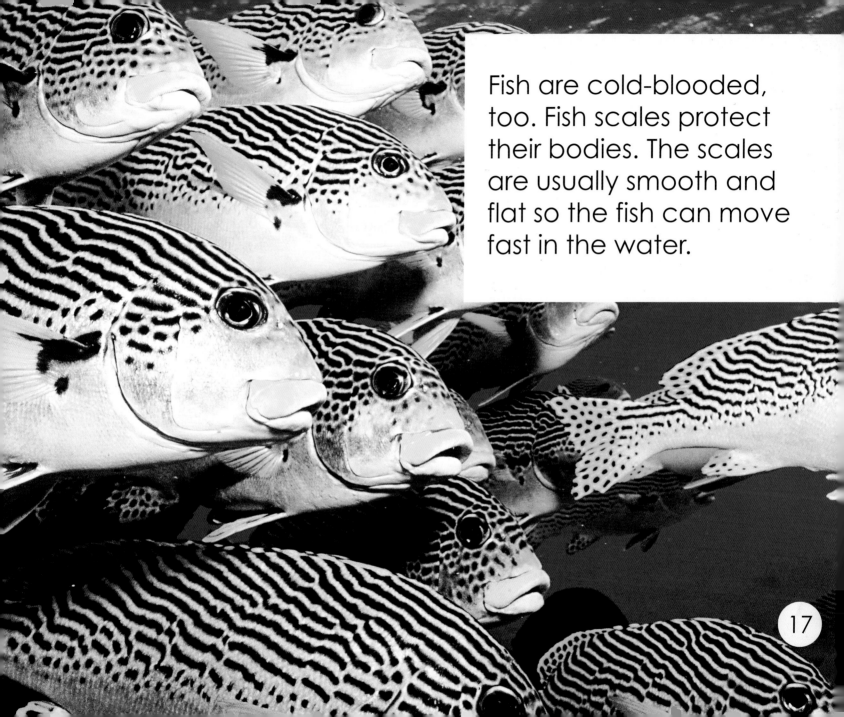

Fish are cold-blooded, too. Fish scales protect their bodies. The scales are usually smooth and flat so the fish can move fast in the water.

Living on land and in water

Animals live on land and in water. Most **mammals**, birds, and **reptiles** live on land. All these animals have **lungs** to breathe **oxygen** from the air.

Fish live in water. Fish have **gills** to take oxygen from the water. This dolphin is a mammal that lives in water.

Q How do dolphins breathe oxygen from the air?

A

Dolphins swim to the surface to breathe in air.

blowhole

 A dolphin takes air into its lungs through a blowhole. The blowhole is on the top of its head. The dolphin pushes air out of its blowhole too.

Some animals called **amphibians** can live on land
and in water. Frogs, toads, and newts are amphibians.
Amphibians lay eggs in water. Their young have **gills**.
The adults have **lungs**.

Eggs and babies

Some animals lay eggs. Birds lay eggs with hard shells. Baby birds grow inside the eggs. The babies break out of the shell when they are big enough.

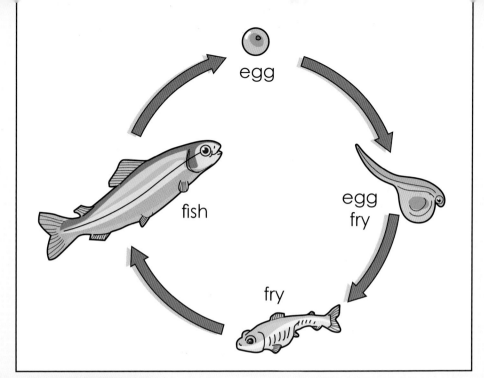

egg

egg
fry

fish

fry

Fish lay hundreds of soft eggs in water. Each tiny egg changes and grows into a baby fish.

Q Do all animals lay eggs?

CLUES

- Do lions lay eggs?
- Does a baby elephant hatch from an egg?

A No, some animals give birth to live young.

Most **mammals** give birth to their babies. Most mammals make milk in their bodies to feed their young.

24

A kangaroo is a mammal that keeps its young in a pouch in its body. When the baby is first born it is tiny. It stays in the pouch until it is big enough to move and find food on its own.

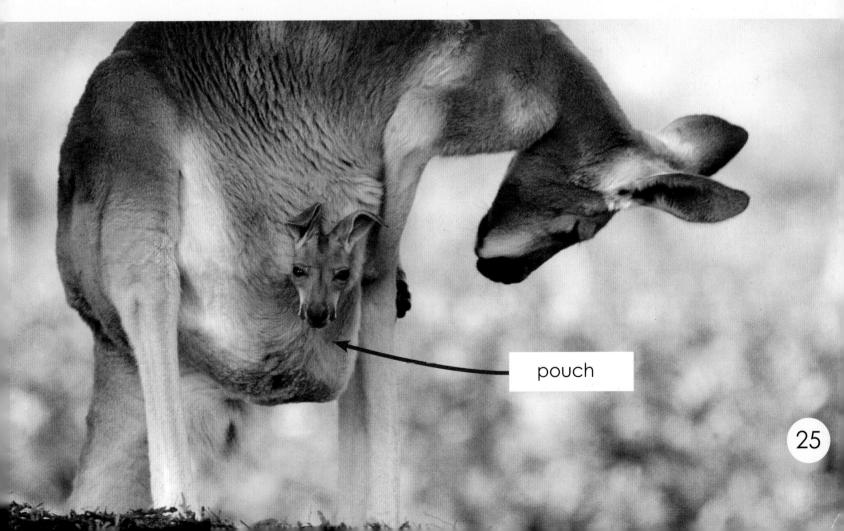

pouch

Other animal groups

There are many other animal groups. One of the biggest groups is **insects**. Insects have six legs and most can fly. Bees, butterflies, beetles, and flies are all insects.

Spiders, snails, crabs, worms, and jellyfish all belong to different animal groups. Each group has different characteristics.

This animal is a jellyfish.

There are many different animal groups. Animals are put into groups because of the characteristics they share. These are some of the animal goups:

Mammals:

➡ are **warm-blooded**

➡ have fur or hair on body

➡ breathe using **lungs**

➡ give birth to live young

➡ feed their young on milk.

Birds:

➡ are warm-blooded

➡ breathe using lungs

➡ have feathers

➡ lay eggs with hard shells

➡ have wings.

Fish:

- are **cold-blooded**
- breathe using **gills**
- have wet scales
- lay eggs in water.

Amphibians:

- are cold-blooded
- have soft skin (no fur or scales)
- lay eggs in water
- live on land and in water.

Reptiles:

- are cold-blooded
- breathe using lungs
- have dry scaly skin
- lay eggs with soft, strong shells.

Checklist

Animals are living things.

A characteristic is something that makes one animal different from another.

Characteristics help animals to:
⇒ breathe
⇒ eat
⇒ move
⇒ grow.

Glossary

amphibian animal that can live on land or in water

cold-blooded not able to keep warm. Cold-blooded animals' bodies are as cold or hot as the air or water around them. They need the warmth of the sun to help them move.

gill part of an animal's body that takes oxygen from water. Fish have gills.

insect animal with six legs and a body with three parts. Ants and beetles are insects.

lung part of an animal's body that takes oxygen from air. Reptiles use lungs to breathe.

mammal animal that gives birth to live young and feeds its young with milk

oxygen gas found in air and water. Animals need oxygen to breathe.

reptile cold-blooded animal that breathes in air. Reptiles usually have scales. Snakes and lizards are reptiles.

scaly covered with scales. Scales are tiny, flat plates that cover some animals' bodies. Fish and reptiles have scales.

warm-blooded able to make its own heat. Warm-blooded animals are warm even if the air around them is cold.

Index

amphibians 21

birds 10, 11–13, 18, 22

cold-blooded animals
   16–17, 29

eggs 22, 23, 28, 29

feathers 4, 5, 10–13, 28
fur 4, 6–8, 28, 29

gills 19, 21, 29

insects 26

mammals 6–7, 9, 18,
   24–25, 28

oxygen 18–19

reptiles 14, 18

scales 14, 17, 29

warm-blooded animals
   7, 13, 28